PICTURE WINDOW BOOKS
a capstone imprint

Editor: Julie Gassman
Designer: Ashlee Suker
Art Director: Nathan Gassman
Production Specialist: Laura Manthe
The illustrations in this book were created with watercolor.

Picture Window Books
1710 Roe Crest Drive
North Mankato, MN 56003
www.capstonepub.com

Library of Congress Cataloging-in-Publication Data
Manushkin, Fran.
  It doesn't need to rhyme, Katie: writing a poem with Katie Woo / by
Fran Manushkin; illustrated by Tammie Lyon.
      p. cm. — (Katie Woo, star writer)
  Includes sidebars about different kinds of poetry and encouragement
on writing about what you feel.
  Summary: Katie and her friends explore writing different kinds of
poetry about themselves and their surroundings.
  ISBN 978-1-4048-8128-0 (library binding)
  ISBN 978-1-4795-1923-1 (paperback.)
  ISBN 978-1-4795-1889-0 (eBook PDF)
1. Woo, Katie (Fictitious character)—Juvenile fiction. 2. Chinese
Americans—Juvenile fiction. 3. Poetry—Authorship—Juvenile fiction.
4. Creative writing—Juvenile fiction. [1. Chinese Americans—Fiction.
2. Poetry—Authorship—Fiction. 3. Creative writing—Fiction.] I. Lyon,
Tammie, ill. II. Title. III. Title: It does not need to rhyme, Katie.

PZ7.M3195It 2013
813.54—dc23   2013004206

Printed in the United States of America.
0405

Katie Woo

star writer

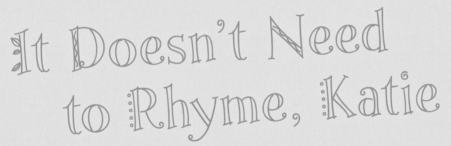

It Doesn't Need to Rhyme, Katie

Writing a Poem with Katie Woo

by Fran Manushkin   illustrated by Tammie Lyon

Katie Woo was jumping rope.

She sang,

>"Roses are red,
>
>Violets are blue,
>
>What's my name?
>
>It's Katie Woo!"

Katie sang her rhyme over and over. She jumped to JoJo's house and sang it to her.

"That's a cool rhyme," said JoJo. "I can do one too."

Katie's Star Tip

My rhyme has a nice rhythm too. The stressed, or louder parts, in the words give each line a steady beat. Tap your foot as you read it, and you'll see what I mean. RO-ses are RED, VIO-lets are BLUE, WHAT'S my NAME? It's KA-tie WOO!

"My name is JoJo.

I can jump high!

I might even jump

Up to the sky!"

"Yay!" yelled Katie.

"I love it!"

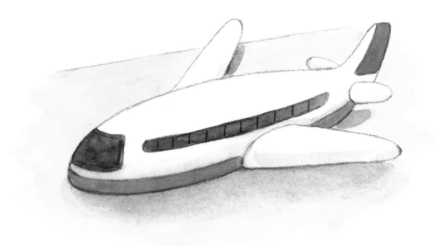

Pedro came by, flying his toy airplane. "My dad's making cookies," he said. "Can you come to my house and have a snack with us?"

"For sure!" said Katie.

Katie, Pedro, and JoJo ate cookie

after cookie after cookie!

"I'd like to write a poem about

these," said Katie. "But I can't find

a rhyme for cookies."

Katie's Star Tip

Try thinking of topics for poems. There are so many things to write about! Look around. Almost anything your eyes spy could become the topic for a poem—even this book.

"Poems don't always have to rhyme," said Pedro. "I wrote a poem about my dad. It's fun and it doesn't rhyme. Want to hear it?"

"Sure!" said Katie.

Pedro read his poem:

"When my dad wakes up,

his face feels scratchy.

After he shaves,

it's smoooooooth!"

"That's great!" Katie smiled. "But is it really a poem?"

"Sure," said Pedro.

"You made up a new word," said JoJo. "You put lots of O's in *smooth*."

"It's fun playing with words," said Pedro.

Just then, it started to rain. The wind blew, and raindrops went plink, plunk on the windows.

JoJo wrote a poem about it:

"I hear the wind blowing

through the trees.

Whish!

Whoosh!

Swoooooooooosh!"

"Wow!" said Katie. "Your words sound like the wind."

Katie's Star Tip

I like poems that play with sounds. JoJo's poem about wind actually sounds like the wind! Miss Winkle says that sound words are called onomatopoeia. I love saying these kinds of words out loud ... *zip, pop, meow, arf, boom, buzz!*

"I like writing happy poems," said
Pedro, "about camping with my dad
and eating hot dogs."

"Sometimes I write sad poems," said JoJo. "It makes me feel better."

"Me too!" said Katie. "But I want to write every kind of poem."

Katie's Star Tip

Lots of poems talk about feelings. Poets use details to explain how it feels to be angry or nervous or proud. Really great poems will make the reader feel the same way.

"I can write about riding on my dad's shoulders," decided Katie. "That always makes me happy. Or I can write a sad poem about the time my dog was sick."

"I'm writing a poem that spells out my name," said Pedro. "Each line will begin with one of the letters."

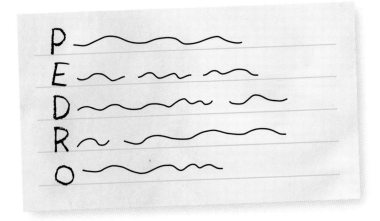

Katie's Star Tip

There are different types of poems. They each have certain rules that make them fun to write. They might have a rhyming pattern or a certain number of syllables in each line. In an acrostic poem, the first letters of each line of the poem combine to form a word. That word is the topic of the poem. Pedro's poem is an acrostic.

Pedro read his poem:

"Pedro is my name.

Every day I like to play soccer.

Doughnuts are my favorite food.

Riding my bike is the most fun.

Oatmeal is NOT my favorite food!"

"That's a cool poem," said Katie.

"Thanks!" Pedro said proudly. "I'm showing it to Miss Winkle tomorrow. She loves my poems."

"I'll bring her a poem too," said Katie.

Katie went home and took out a pencil and paper.

"Miss Winkle said poems can be about what we see," said Katie. "Or what we hear or touch or smell or taste."

Katie's Star Tip

When I write using my senses, it helps readers imagine that they are seeing, hearing, touching, smelling, or tasting the same things as me. It's like they are entering a special world that I made up!

"I could write about playing with JoJo's soft kitten," said Katie. "Or jumping in messy mud, or watching noisy fireworks, or tasting hot, salty french fries."

"There's so much to write about!" sighed Katie. "I don't know what to choose."

"It's time for your bath," called Katie's mom.

"Oh, no," moaned Katie. "I don't have a poem yet!"

Katie sat in the soft, sweet

bubbles. Suddenly she shouted,

"I know what to write about, but I

don't have a pencil."

"Tell it to me," said Katie's mom,

"and I will write it down."

The next day in class, Pedro read

his poem.

"It's terrific!" praised Miss Winkle.

JoJo read her poem about

the wind.

"That's great too!" said

Miss Winkle.

Then Katie read her poem:

"My bubble bath is warm and tickly.

The bubbles buzz and smell sweet.

I am wearing a pretty white gown.

Look! I am a princess."

Katie's Star Tip

My poem uses comparisons called metaphors.
I didn't really wear a gown in the bathtub. I was just
sitting in bubbles. I am not really a princess, but I
felt like one! Saying I was a princess in a white gown
is more interesting and fun than just writing that
I was a girl in a bubble bath.

"Your poem is splendid!" praised Miss Winkle.

"Writing it made me happy!" Katie smiled. "And this time, it didn't have to rhyme!"

Poems of Your Own!

Now that you've learned some things about poetry, try writing your own. It's so much fun! Here are some ideas.

✿ Write an acrostic poem with friends. Together, choose a word and write it going up and down, like Pedro did with his name. Then each of you take turns writing a line!

✿ Use metaphors to describe each member of your family. Put them together for a poem your parents will love!

✿ Write a poem about your favorite animal, and make the lines rhyme at the end.

Glossary

acrostic—a poem in which the first letters of each line spell out a word or phrase

metaphor—a figure of speech that compares two different things

onomatopoeia—words that copy the sound they are describing, such as *hiss*

rhyme—word endings that sound the same

rhythm—a pattern of beats, like in music

senses—one of the ways a person learns about surroundings; the five senses are sight, hearing, touch, taste, and smell

syllable—a small unit of language that includes a vowel sound; a syllable is like a beat of music

topic—what your poem is about

Read More

Freese, Susan M. *Guppies to Puppies: Reading, Writing, and Reciting Poems About Pets.* Poetry Power. Edina, Minn.: ABDO Pub. Co., 2008.

Loewen, Nancy. *Words, Wit, and Wonder: Writing Your Own Poem.* Writer's Toolbox. Minneapolis: Picture Window Books, 2009.

Prelutsky, Jack. *Pizza, Pigs, and Poetry: How to Write a Poem.* New York: Greenwillow Books, 2008.

On the Internet

✿ Learn more about Katie and her friends.

✿ Find a Katie Woo color sheet, scrapbook, and stationery.

✿ Discover more Katie Woo books.

All at ... www.capstonekids.com

Still Want More?
Find cool websites related to this book at *www.facthound.com.*

Just type in this code: **9781404881280** and you're ready to go!

About the Author

Fran Manushkin is the author of many popular picture books, including *Baby, Come Out!*; *Latkes and Applesauce: A Hanukkah Story*; *The Tushy Book*; *The Belly Book*; and *Big Girl Panties*. There is a real Katie Woo—she's Fran's great-niece—but she never gets in half the trouble of the Katie Woo in the books. Fran writes on her beloved Mac computer in New York City, without the help of her two naughty cats, Chaim and Goldy.

About the Illustrator

Tammie Lyon began her love for drawing at a young age while sitting at the kitchen table with her dad. She continued her love of art and eventually attended the Columbus College of Art and Design, where she earned a bachelor's degree in fine art. Today she lives with her husband, Lee, in Cincinnati, Ohio. Her dogs, Gus and Dudley, keep her company as she works in her studio.

Look for all the books in the series:

It Doesn't Need to Rhyme, Katie

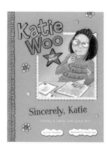

Sincerely, Katie

Stick to the Facts, Katie

What Do You Think, Katie?

What Happens Next, Katie?

What's in Your Heart, Katie?